This book belongs to:

____

Made in United States
Orlando, FL
07 November 2022

24307060R00065